Chocolate, Chocolate, Everywhere!

Written by Paul Mason

Illustrated by Russ Daff

Chocolate, chocolate, everywhere

All over the world, people eat chocolate. Chocolate is a very popular food.

This picture shows a man making chocolate many years ago!

Chocolate comes in different flavours. It also comes in different shapes and sizes.

The cocoa tree

The cocoa tree is sometimes called the chocolate tree. The cocoa tree comes from Central and South America.

The cocoa tree grows fruit. Inside the fruit are cocoa beans. These are used to make chocolate.

How to make chocolate

First, people pick the cocoa beans.

They leave the beans for a few days. Then, they dry the beans in the sun.

Next, the beans go into a machine to cook them. It's very hot.

The shells come off the cocoa beans.

Another machine presses the beans and makes a brown liquid.

After the beans are pressed, the chocolate maker adds milk and sugar and then mixes.

Then, the chocolate maker makes chocolates in different shapes!

Different types of chocolate

Dark chocolate has got a very strong flavour. It's got a lot of cocoa in it.

Milk chocolate is sweet. It's made from milk and sugar mixed with cocoa.

White chocolate is made from a different part of cocoa beans. It's called cocoa butter.

Is chocolate good for you?

Some people say that eating chocolate is good for you! Chocolate helps to keep your heart healthy.

But eating too much chocolate can be bad for you. Some chocolate has got a lot of sugar. This is bad for your teeth.

Hooray for chocolate!

Chocolate is a nice treat! On special days, people give presents. Some people give chocolates to celebrate.

People have chocolate at parties. Sometimes there are chocolate fountains.

Recipe for chocolate sauce

Make sure there is an adult to help you!

INGREDIENTS

200g dark chocolate

70g sugar

100ml cream

50ml water

DIRECTIONS:

- Put all the ingredients into a bowl.
- Boil some water in a saucepan. Be careful!
- Put the bowl on top of the saucepan. It needs to be above the water.
- Stir the chocolate until it melts.
- Dip some strawberries and bananas in and enjoy!

The Chocolate Fountain

Written by Paul Mason
Illustrated by Russ Daff

Mr and Mrs Hall and their son, James, are at the train station. They are in a new town.

There aren't a lot of shops in this town. Everybody goes to the big supermarket.

The shop is empty. The Hall family are opening a new shop. It's a chocolate shop.

The Hall family work hard. They clean, they sweep and they paint.

Mr Hall makes a new sign for the shop. It says, *Tasty Chocolates*.

Mr and Mrs Hall make a lot of chocolates. They put the chocolates on the shelves in the new shop.

A man comes into the shop. He looks angry.

The man laughs at their small shop. He doesn't think they can sell much chocolate.

The man owns the big supermarket in town. His name is Mr Nelson.

James starts to worry. He thinks about how many chocolates *Tasty Chocolates* can sell.

Mr and Mrs Hall have got a plan. They've got a special machine.

Mrs Hall uses her special chocolate sauce recipe. She mixes the chocolate. She pours it into the fountain.

The fountain looks amazing! The chocolate pours down.

The smell from the chocolate fountain travels all over the town. The police officer, vet and shop assistant can all smell the chocolate.

Soon the shop is full of customers. They all want a tasty chocolate treat.

The Hall family are very busy.

Mr Nelson smells the chocolate.

He sees that the new chocolate shop is full.
He sees the happy customers.

Mr Nelson eats some chocolate from the chocolate fountain.

Everybody eats more chocolate. Everybody is very happy that the Hall family are here.

Activities

1 Complete the sentences.

popular America flavours sugar ~~cocoa~~

1 Chocolate is made from ___cocoa___ beans.
2 Milk chocolate has got milk and ______ mixed in it.
3 The cocoa tree comes from Central and South ______.
4 Chocolate comes in different ______.
5 Chocolate is a very ______ food.

2 Label the picture using words from the box.

~~police officer~~ vet shop assistant fountain customer

3 Unscramble the words. Then match them to the pictures.

1 e v t ____vet____
2 p h o s ________
3 n a i t o u f n ________
4 l o c h o c a e t ________

4 Circle *T* (True) or *F* (False).

1 The cocoa tree is sometimes called the chocolate tree. (T) F
2 Dark chocolate has got a lot of cocoa. T F
3 Chocolate is made from cocoa beans. T F
4 Inside the cocoa fruit there are tiny chocolates. T F
5 Milk chocolate has got milk and sugar mixed in it. T F

5 Who says it? Match the speech bubbles to the characters.

1 In fact, I love it!

2 Our fountain!

3 Great sign, Dad.

4 Let's sweep the floor.

5 I've got a bigger shop than you!

6 Our shop looks lovely.

6 Write the answers to these questions. Choose the answers from the box.

It's chocolate! Yes, you can. ~~Yes, I am.~~
Go straight on.

1 Are you the owner of this shop? Yes, I am.

2 Can I have some chocolate from the fountain, please?

____

3 Where's this shop? ________________

4 What's that delicious smell? ________________

7 Put the story in the correct order. Write the numbers.

- [ ] The smell from the chocolate fountain travels all over town.
- [ ] Mr Nelson is sorry he wasn't nice.
- [ ] The new chocolate shop is full of customers.
- [ ] The Hall family work hard.
- [ ] Mr Nelson laughs at their small shop.
- [ ] James gives Mr Nelson some chocolate to eat.
- [1] Mr and Mrs Hall and their son, James, are at the train station.

8 Match the sentences to the pictures.

1 A machine presses the beans into a brown liquid.

2 The chocolate maker makes chocolates in different shapes.

3 The shells come off the cocoa beans.

4 People pick the cocoa beans.

a 

b 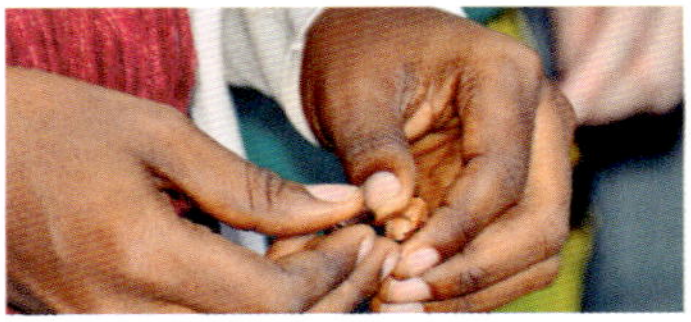

c 

d 

9 Put the words in the correct order to make sentences.

1 chocolates people Some give celebrate to

Some people give chocolates to celebrate ______________________.

2 beans the Inside fruit cocoa are

____.

3 grows The fruit cocoa tree

____.

4 presses A machine liquid and makes the beans a brown

____.

10 Complete the crossword and find the secret word.

1 

2 

3 

4 

	1 s	i	g	n										
2														
3														
	4						■							

The secret word is: ___ ___ ___ ___

Picture Dictionary

world

cocoa tree

fruit

cocoa beans

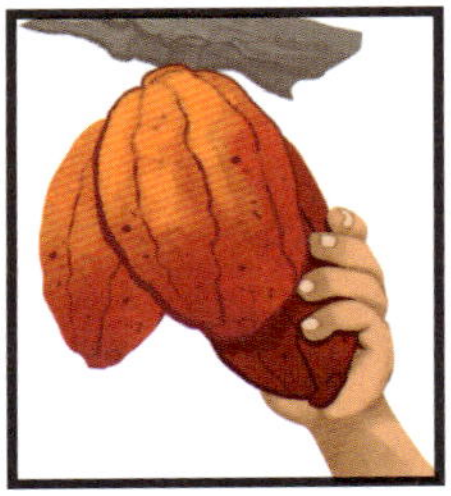
pick (v)

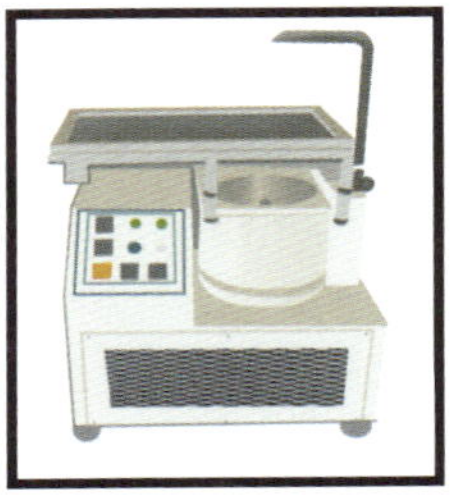
machine

shell

liquid

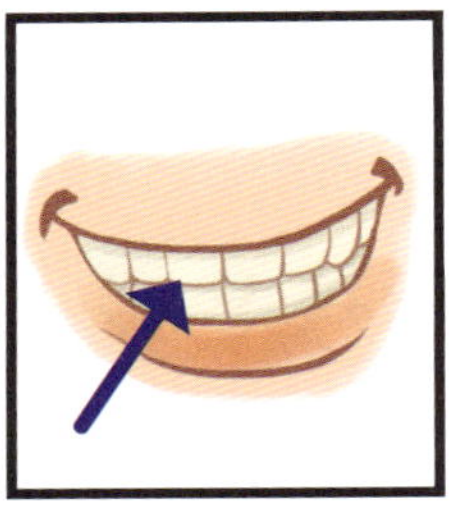
teeth

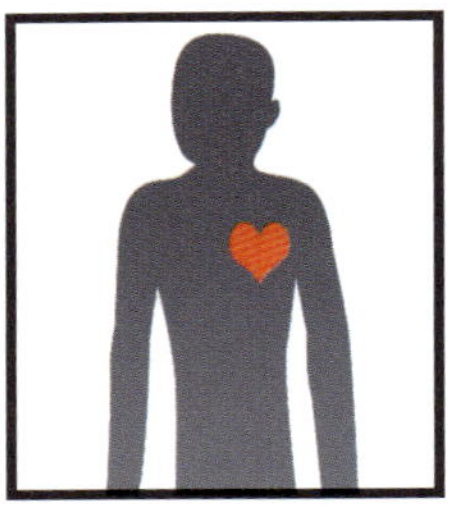
heart

present

fountain

bowl

saucepan

stir (v)

melt (v)

train station

town

shop

newsagent's

supermarket

sweep (v)

sign

shelf

money

sauce

recipe

smell (v)

police officer

vet

shop assistant

customer

Macmillan Education
4 Crinan Street
London N1 9XW
A division of Springer Nature Limited
Companies and representatives throughout the world

ISBN 978-1-3800-3838-8

Written by Paul Mason

First published 2015
This edition published 2019

Designed by Carolyn Gibson
Illustrated by Russ Daff
Cover photograph by **Alamy**/ImageBroker
Picture research by Emily Taylor

The authors and publishers would like to thank the following for permission to reproduce their photographs: **Alamy**/Rafael Ben-Ari p6(br), Alamy/Sabena Jane Blackbird p3(cr), Alamy/Blend Images p9(tr), Alamy/Bon Appetit p4(br), Alamy/ImageBroker p3(picking cocoa), Alamy/Darrin Jenkins pp6(bl), 28(d), Alamy/SnapperUK pp4(t), 28(a): **Corbis**/2/Tom Le Goff/Ocean p8(bl), Corbis/Macduff Everton pp5(b) p28(c); **Getty Images** p10(bananas), Getty Images p7, Getty Images/AWL Images pp5(t), Getty Images/Digital Vision Vectors/ duncan1890 p2(tr), Getty Images/Newton Daly p8(t), Getty Images/Dorling Kindersley p10(t), Getty Images/Lonely Planet Images p6(t), Getty Images/lucio pepi/FOAP p28(b), Getty Images/Gavin Parsons p4(bl); **Studio8** p10(strawberries); **SuperStock** p2(b); **ThinkStock**/ iStock/Pablo Gonzalez Poncela p9(bl).

Printed and bound in Great Britain by Bell and Bain Ltd, Glasgow

2023 2022 2021 2020 2019
10 9 8 7 6 5 4 3 2 1